PATIENCE

Robin Jackson

Haldane **Mason**

First published in the UK in 2001 by
Haldane Mason Ltd
59 Chepstow Road
London W2 5BP
email: haldane.mason@dial.pipex.com

ISBN: 1-902463-79-X

A HALDANE MASON BOOK

Art Director: Ron Samuel
Editor: Kate Latham
Designers: Rachel Clark, Phil Ford

Colour reproduction by CK Midas

Printed in China

Contents

Introduction

Welcome to the excitement and challenge of Patience! This great family of one-person card games offers amusement and interest on a wide range of levels to suit your mood, taste and ability. All you need is a standard pack of playing cards – or sometimes two packs – and a table.

All Patience games are based on the fact that a standard pack of 52 cards can be rearranged in many different ways – 2,704 different ways, to be precise. Two packs, making 104 cards, can be rearranged in 10,816 ways. Most of these sequences will be random ones.

The art of Patience is to start with a randomly arranged pack, or packs, and then rearrange the cards into a specific sequence by following certain rules. It is these different rules which make all the forms of Patience possible. Most often, the aim is to end up with the cards separated into their respective suits and arranged in the correct numerical sequence within the suit, either in ascending or descending order. But there are many other possible aims.

This book assumes no previous knowledge of card games on your part. Already you will have come across a technical term, the 'suit'. With all the other vocabulary of Patience, this term is clearly explained in the list of technical terms on pages 7–9. But here are some basic details that you will need to understand before you start playing.

The pack of 52 cards is divided into four sets of 13 cards, known as suits. Each suit has its own special symbol. Two are black in colour: Clubs and Spades. Two are red in colour: Hearts and Diamonds. Each suit has a group of three 'honour' or 'court' cards – King, Queen and Jack – and nine number cards, from Ten down to Two. The Ace can be treated as the highest card ('Ace high') or as the lowest card ('Ace low'): its value in each game is made clear. In addition, the standard pack has two extra cards, with a jester symbol. These are known as the Jokers. The Patience games described in this book do not use the Jokers.

Some Patience games are completely dependent on chance. If the cards fall right, you will win; if they don't, you will lose. Others are more contingent on how you play the cards: if you make the right choices, you could win. Some games depend on your ability to remember, or to see patterns developing. The demands made on your brain can range from virtually zero to a serious intellectual struggle at the level of a Chess grandmaster. For each game, the chance of working out successfully is shown as Odds: Against, Odds: Favourable, or Odds: Even. The first means that, more often than not, the player fails to complete the game. The second means that, more often than not, the player does

complete the game. Evens mean the player has a fifty-fifty chance. You will soon find out that favourable odds do not necessarily mean that a game is any easier to work out. Some games in which the odds are unfavourable are quite simple games: it just means that the element of luck is greater.

Although the essence of Patience is that you can and do play it on your own, this does not mean that you do not have an opponent. Your opponent is the cards, which all too often do not do what you want them to. In this respect, playing Patience is really no different to other competitive card games, in which there are always winners and losers. If you

play Bridge or Poker, and lose, you are unlikely to say you will never play again (unless you lose your shirt as well as the game). In the same way, Patience players should not expect to win every time. Sometimes it just doesn't work out. Don't let this discourage you. Of Patience it can truly be said that: 'To travel hopefully is better than to arrive.'

Patience card games have been around since the late eighteenth century. The earliest ones seem to have come from the north of Europe – around the Baltic coastline of Germany, Poland, and the south of Scandinavia – a region which has also produced such famous competitive card games as Skat. Patience soon spread to France, and it was there that most of the technical terms of the game were formalized, and its

two names of Patience and Solitaire were introduced. In the 200 years or so that Patience has been played, many different games have been developed, and new forms are always being invented.

Some of the most common games are known by several names around the world. Bernard Shaw's remark, that England and America are two nations divided by a common language, could have been made with Patience in mind. Canfield in the UK is Klondike in the US, while Canfield in the US is Demon in the UK.

Most of the early terms in Patience come from French and are still found in use, though there are English alternatives. The layout can be referred to as the 'tableau' and the stock pile may be called the 'talon'. In this book we use the terms that are self-explanatory as far as possible, but if you're unsure of any term, you can look it up on the following pages.

Technical Terms

Ace high: Ace is the top scoring card.

Ace low: Ace is the lowest scoring card.

Alternating colours: Placing a red card (a Heart or Diamond card) on a black card (a Club or Spade card), or a black card on a red card, and so on, in sequence.

Available card: A card ready to be used in the course of play.

Base card: Another word for a Foundation card.

Block: A stage in a game when the player cannot make any further move, although the game is not completed.

Build up: Laying cards in ascending order of value on top of a Foundation card.

Build down: Laying the cards in descending order of value on top of a Foundation card.

Column: Cards laid on the table often overlapping, extending towards the player.

Court cards: Kings, Queens and Jacks.

Deal: Passing out cards for play. Dealing can be with the cards face-up, or face-down.

Deck: Another word for Pack.

Discard: To play a card to the waste pile.

Downcard: A card lying face-down.

Exposed card: The top card of a pile or column, lying with its face fully visible. An Exposed card is normally also an Available one.

File: A column with cards overlapping but with suits and Pip values visible. Files are extended towards the player.

Follow suit: To play a card of the same Suit as the card previously played.

Foundation card: A card placed face-up on which other cards are built up or down. They are normally Aces or Kings. *Also known as* a Base card.

Foundation pile: A stack of cards assembled on top of a Foundation card, in a specified sequence.

Foundation row: A side-by-side row of Foundation cards.

Grace: A special move allowed in some games, usually only once per game, to release a Block.

Hand: That part of the Pack which has not been dealt out. *Also known as* the Stock.

Honour cards: Kings, Queens and Jacks.

Layout: The specified way in which the cards are set out in individual games. *Also known as* the Tableau.

Number card: Card of any value between 10 and 2. *Also known as* a Pip card or Spot card.

Overlap: Placing cards in a column so that they partly cover each other, but the Suit and value of each card can still be clearly seen.

Pack: A full set of playing cards.

Packet: Set of cards that is less than a full Pack.

Pair: Two cards of the same rank, e.g. two Eights, two Jacks.

Pile: Cards stacked in such a way that only the top card is visible, whether face-up or face-down.

Pip card: Card of any value between 10 and 2. *Also known as* a Number card or Spot card.

Pip value: The number on a Number card (e.g. a Nine has nine pips).

Play: To play a card is to take it up and use it in the game.

Rank: The value of a card.

Re-deal: Using the cards from the Waste pile to deal again, when the Stock is used up.

Reserve: A row of overlapping cards of which the top one is available for play.

Row: A line of cards placed side by side (Suit and Pip value must always be visible if cards overlap).

Sequence: The ranking order in which the cards run, from high to low, or the other way round. It also applies to a group of cards placed in a specific ranking order. A sequence can be strictly numerical, as 7, 8, 9, 10, J, Q, K irrespective of suit, or numerical with alternating red and black cards. The sequence may be upwards or downwards.

Shuffle: To mix the cards in the Pack thoroughly into a random sequence.

Singleton: A single card of any Suit.

Solitaire: An alternative term for Patience, used in the US and many other countries.

Space: A gap in the Layout, from which a card has been moved.

Spot card: Card of any value between 10 and 2. Also called a Number card or Pip card.

Stack: Another word for Pile.

Stacked: Stacked cards are cards placed in a Pile.

Stock: The cards remaining after dealing, sometimes also called the Hand.

Stock pile: The Stock, when placed face-down on the table in a pile. *Also known as* Talon.

Suit: One of the four sets of cards in a Pack, with the signs of Clubs, Hearts, Spades and Diamonds.

Tableau: Another word for Layout.

Talon: Another word for Stock Pile.

Upcard: A card lying face-up.

Waste pile: A pile of those cards turned up in the course of a game that cannot be placed in the Layout or a Foundation pile. The Waste pile is normally stacked face-up, and its top card is available for play.

Getting Started

All you need is a good-sized table or work surface to lay the cards out on, though it is possible to find special Patience cards in a smaller size (these can also be useful for other card games when travelling).

Note: All games should be played from a thoroughly shuffled pack. Where two packs are specified, shuffle both into a single combined pack, unless the Procedure details for the game say otherwise.

The Games

The Patience games in this book are of two basic types. The first games in the book are those where the aim of play is to reduce the cards to a set layout or arrangement or to group the cards into piles of certain values. The later games involve building sequences of cards according to value and perhaps suit.

The games include both classic games and new games from around the world. Easier Patience games tend to be at the front of the book but there are some wonderfully challenging games later for you to pit your wits against the cards.

The Queen and Her Lad

This is a very simple Patience game, which depends entirely on chance.

Aim: *To remove all cards except the Queen and the Jack of Hearts.*

Odds: *Against*

Procedure: Use a single pack of 52 cards. Remove the Queen and Jack of Hearts, then shuffle the pack. Now place the Queen of Hearts at the top of the pack and the Jack of Hearts at the bottom.

Play: Start dealing out the cards one by one, face-up, from left to right. The Queen of Hearts will be the first card dealt, the Jack the card at the bottom of the pack. As you deal, look for any singleton that lies between two cards of either the same suit, or the same rank, as each other, and take it out, placing it face-up in a waste pile. Also, look for any pair of cards of the same suit or rank that lie side by side between two other cards which are of the same suit or rank as each other, and discard the two middle cards. Close up the row and look again to see if, as a result, you can remove other cards. Then resume dealing, until discarding again becomes possible. You win if you can discard all the cards separating the Queen and her lad.

Discard

Discard

Accordion

Although this is a simple game, it involves an interesting element of decision-making.

Aim: *To end the game with all the cards in one pile.*
Odds: *Against*

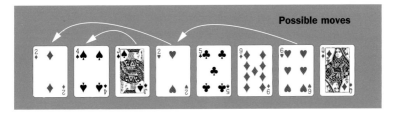

Possible moves

Procedure: Use a single 52-card pack. Deal out all the cards, face-up, in a single row, not overlapping.
Play: You can then move cards as follows: Move a card on to the card on its left, if it is of the same suit or the same rank. Move a card on to the third card to the left, if it is of the same suit or rank.

After making each move, look to see if additional moves are now possible as a result. When cards are stacked, don't just move the topmost card, but the whole stack, according to the value or suit of the topmost card.
Comment: It seems simple, but the odds are against you. If you finish with three piles, you can feel pleased; with two, even more so. With one – you have triumphed against the odds.
Variant: To increase the difficulty, restrict the movable cards to matching suit only.

Aces Up

Another game that is easy to play but hard to resolve.

Aim: *To be left with only the four Aces.*
Odds: *Against*

Procedure: Use a single 52-card pack. Cards rank in descending order from Ace to Two (Aces are high). Deal four cards in a row, face-up.
Play: If two or more cards of the same suit are dealt, discard the low or lower ones, leaving a space. Deal a further four cards face-up on top of the first ones, including the space(s). Again, discard the lower exposed cards of a duplicated suit. An eliminated card may uncover another that can also now be eliminated. Once six deals have been made, you can move the top card or cards of any pile into a space, before the next deal. The aim is to discard all cards except the four Aces, so that you finish with a row of four Aces.
Note: If a discard is at the top of a pile, only the top card is discarded.

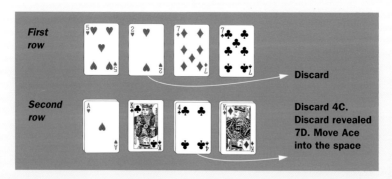

First row

Discard

Second row

Discard 4C.
Discard revealed
7D. Move Ace
into the space

Eighteens

This game is one of several in which the cards must be ordered into pairs or sets, where the combined face value of each pair or set adds up to a particular total.

Aim: *To create 24 sets of cards, each set with a face value of 18.*
Odds: *Against*

Procedure: Use two 52-card packs. Remove the Aces as they are not required in the game. Deal out two rows of six cards, face-up.
Play: Look at the cards you have dealt. If you can find any set(s) of four cards, comprising three different number cards which together total 18 (e.g. 9, 6, 3) plus a court card, take them out as a set. Suit does not matter.

Deal further cards to fill the gaps in the layout, then remove any more sets. Continue in this way until you cannot form any further sets.

Now deal a further 12 cards, laying them face-up on top of the cards in the

First set removed (shadowed cards)

layout. Form sets as before. Exposed cards from earlier deals can be used. Continue to deal and sort until both packs have been fully dealt. At this point, either you can complete the game, or you have lost.
Note 1: Only number cards from Two to Ten count; court cards have no value, but there must be one court card in each of the 24 piles.
Note 2: Cards may not be moved within the layout.

Clock Patience

This is a very simple Patience game, which depends entirely on chance.

Aim: *To arrange all the cards in a clock-face formation, with Kings in the centre.*

Odds: *Against*

Procedure: Use a single 52-card pack. Deal 13 packets of four cards, face-down in a circle, like numbers on a clock face, with one packet in the centre as the stock pile. Turn the top card of the stock pile face-up. Queens count as 12, Jacks as 11, Aces as one; number cards take their pip values. The aim is to

place all the cards in the right place on the 'clock'; e.g. all four Sixes at six o'clock; all four Queens at 12 o'clock.

Play: Place the top card from the stock in its correct position, face-up under the packet, and turn over the top card of that packet. Place that card in its right place, and so on. If you turn over a King, place it face-up at the bottom of the stock pile, and turn over the top card on the stock pile. You win if the last card to be turned up is the fourth King, because by then you will have completed the clock.

Ninety-One

A counting game which can be resolved in more than one way.

Aim: *To achieve a layout with a pip value of 91 exactly.*
Odds: *Favourable*

Procedure: Use a single 52-card pack, and deal out 13 piles, each of four cards, face-up. Calculate the total value of the top cards showing in the layout. Each number card is worth its pip value. Aces count as one, Jacks count as 11, Queens 12, and Kings 13. If you have dealt out 91 – congratulations! More probably, you will have to do some moving around of cards. All top cards are available, and can be moved to the top of any other pile. But each pile must retain at least one card.

The most elegant and difficult solution is to form a complete sequence from Ace to King, which just happens to add up to 91. But there are other ways of reaching the total, one of which is shown here.

Note: Some players set themselves a time-limit for this game. Can you beat the clock as well as the cards?

A layout adding up to 91

Golf

Sometimes called Fan Tan. A popular game, though the odds are in favour of the cards. Despite the name, the effect is more like putting than a round of golf. If you regard the base pile as the equivalent of the 'hole' then you want to 'putt' each card into it.

Aim: *To completely clear the hand on to the base card or 'putt' the hand into the hole.*

Odds: *Against*

Procedure: Use a single 52-card pack. Deal a row of seven cards, face-up. Deal four more rows, face-up on top of the first row, overlapping so that you can see the value of each card in each column of five. This forms the hand.

Deal one more card, face-up, and place it separately, as a base on which to build. Place the remaining cards in a pile, face-up, below it, to form the stock.

Play: You may now take cards from the hand, or the top card of the stock, to place on the base card or hole. But each card must be in sequence to the card it goes on, either upwards or downwards. Suit and colour do not matter, only the rank of the card.

Aces are low, and only a Two may be placed on top of an Ace. Kings end a sequence. If you have only a King to play, then, after placing the King on the end of a sequence, draw the next card from the stock – whatever its value – and place it on top of the King. Then carry on as before. You also do this if there is no playable card available in the hand or the stock.

Hand

Hole

Stock

Play can start with 5S or 5D, but 5S frees 4C and 5D can then be played, followed by 6C, 7H, 8C (exposing a new top card on the stock), 9S, 10D, JH, and so on

If you exhaust the stock pile before emptying the hand, and there is no playable card in the hand, you have lost the game.

Variant: In another form of this game, the player is allowed to build a Queen (but not an Ace) on to a King, and continue play.

Monte Carlo

This game is also known as Double or Quits. It is a very simple game which depends purely on chance.

Aim: *To pair off all cards of the same rank.*
Odds: *Against*

Procedure: From a single pack of 52 cards, deal four rows of five cards, face-up.

Play: Take out any pairs, regardless of suit – e.g. Five of Hearts and Five of Clubs – so long as they are next to each other in the layout, whether horizontally, vertically, or diagonally. Stack the pairs in a waste pile, face-up.

Close up the resulting gaps in the layout, keeping the cards in the sequence in which they were dealt (so that a gap on the right-hand side of a row is filled by the first left-hand card of the next row). Then deal such further cards as are necessary to complete the layout of 20 cards. Once again, take out any pairs.

Continue in the same way until you have paired off all the cards, or have come to a block. If you do manage to pair off all the cards, you can feel very pleased, as you will have managed to succeed against the odds.

First deal

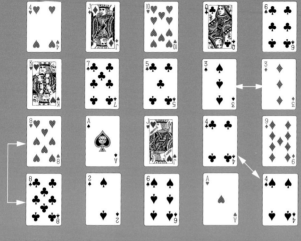

Remove
arrowed
pairs

Second deal

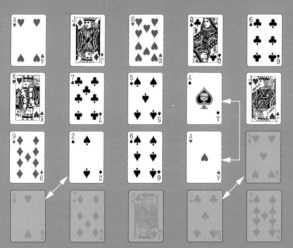

Shaded
cards are
newly dealt.

Remove
arrowed
pairs

Tower of Pisa

Aim: *To end with a single column of cards descending in sequence from Ten to Two.*

Odds: *Favourable*

Procedure: Use a single 52-card pack, and remove one each of the nine number cards, making a complete sequence from Ten to Two, in any mixture of suits. Shuffle the nine cards well. Lay them out in three columns of three cards. Discard the rest of the pack – it is not required. Once this is done, you can start moving cards.

Play: Only the bottom card of a column can be moved, and it can only be moved to the bottom of another column, and under a card of higher value. An empty column can be filled by the bottom card of either of the other two columns.

Note: If you start with a Ten on the bottom row, try to use all the cards from one of the columns, in order to have an empty column. Now you can move the Ten to the top (so long as it is still at the bottom of its original column after your previous moves).

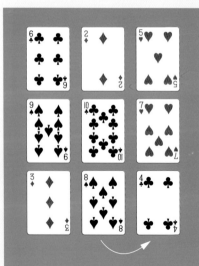

Forty-Nine

Aim: *To build up suits in sequence from Aces to Kings.*
Odds: *Against*

Procedure: Use two 52-card packs. Deal 49 cards face-up in seven rows of seven, to make seven files. This is the layout. The undealt cards become the stock, which is placed face-down.

Play: Turn over the top card of the stock. If it is an Ace, play it as a foundation card, or if not, on to the layout, if it can be added to the exposed card of a column. Sequences on the layout are made in descending sequence and in alternating colour. Any other exposed cards in the layout may also be played, though sequences cannot be moved between columns. If an entire column becomes empty, any available card or sequence (in this instance only) may be moved to fill it.

There is no re-deal in Forty-Nine, but there is a grace. A foundation pile in the course of building may be moved, as a whole only, on to an exposed card in any column, as if it were a single card. The suit does not matter. Cards in descending sequence can then be placed on the pile, in the usual way. The cards placed on the pile can only be moved singly, but when you uncover the pile itself, you can move it back to the foundation pile as though it were a single card.

Foundation piles

Exposed layout cards

Stock

Foundation pile topped by 10C can be moved to JH. 9C and 8H can then be put on it, exposing the next card in columns 5 and 6

Crescent

Aim: *To make eight suit sequences, ascending from the Aces and descending from the Kings.*

Odds: *Favourable*

Procedure: Use two 52-card packs. Extract the Aces and Kings from one of the packs and lay them out in a row as foundation cards. Shuffle the remaining cards thoroughly with the other pack. Deal out the shuffled cards in 16 packets of six, arranged in a crescent

formation to embrace the foundation cards. (You may have to adapt the shape slightly, as below, if your table or playing area is not large enough.) Each packet should be spread or fanned so that the suit and value of each card can be seen.

Play: The exposed card of each packet is available for play. Move cards to the 16 foundation piles as appropriate.

When no further moves are possible, transfer the bottom card in each packet to the top, then resume play. This transfer from bottom to top may be done up to three times.

Note: Cards may not be transferred from the foundation piles, once placed there.

Betsy Ross

This game is named after the lady who cut out the stars for the first US flag, with one clever snip of her scissors for each star. The dexterity required here is in mental arithmetic.

Aim: *To build up suites in special sequences, irrespective of suit, from four foundation cards.*

Odds: *Against*

Procedure: Use one 52-card pack. Lay any Ace, Two, Three and Four face-up in a row. Place any Two, Four, Six and Eight below the first four cards, with the Two below the Ace, and so on. These are your foundation cards. The top row are indicator cards, to remind you of the numerical intervals in the foundation piles. These run as follows: Below the Ace:

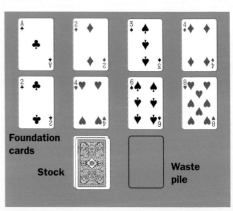

2, 3, 4, 5, 6, 7, 8, 9, 10, J, Q, K, A. Below the Two: 4, 6, 8, 10, Q, A, 3, 5, 7, 9, J, K, 2. Below the Three: 6, 9, Q, 2, 5, 8, J, A, 4, 7, 10, K, 3. Below the Four: 8, Q, 3, 7, J, 2, 6, 10, A, 5, 9, K, 4.

Play: Lay the pack face-down, as the stock. If cards cannot be played to any foundation pile, place them face-up on a waste pile, where the top card is also available for play. When the stock is used up, turn over the waste pile to form a new stock pile. You may do this twice.

Beleaguered Castle

Aim: *To build up four piles in suit and sequence, from Ace (low) to King.*

Odds: *Against*

Procedure: Use a single 52-card pack. Take out the four Aces and arrange them in a column (not overlapping). These are your foundation cards. The layout is made by dealing six cards on either side of each of the Aces, alternately left and right, face-up, in overlapping rows.

Play: Only the outermost card in each of these rows is

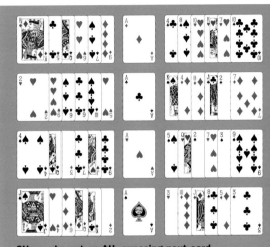

2H may be put on AH, exposing next card
9S may be put on 10C, exposing next card
3C may be put on 4S, exposing next card
10C may be put on JS, exposing next card

available. These can be placed on one of the Aces if they form the next card in suit and sequence. Alternatively, they can be placed at the outer end of another row, but only in sequence of descending pip value; the suit does not matter. For example, you can place a Five of Hearts on a Six of Spades. If a row becomes empty, any available card may be placed in it. In this way, cards can be moved around, but this is still a very tricky game to complete successfully.

Snail

The fun of this game comes from the layout. It is a fairly straightforward Patience with favourable odds.

Aim: *To build sequences downwards in suit from Fives and upwards from Sixes.*

Odds: *Favourable*

Procedure: Use two packs of 52 cards. Remove all the Fives, Sixes and Jacks, and arrange them in a spiral, starting in the centre with the Fives, then Sixes, then Jacks, all face-up, in Diamonds–Clubs–Hearts–Spades order. Below your 'snail', deal four cards from the pack on their long side, face-up. This is the reserve. Turn the combined pack face-down to form the stock.

Play: Move cards as you can on to the Fives and Sixes. Use them as foundation cards and remember that from the Fives you build down (i.e. the next card is a Four of the same suit) and that from the Sixes you build up (i.e. the next card is a Seven of the same suit). The Ace precedes the King when building down from a Five, and follows the King when building up from a Six.

You may play cards from the reserve or, if none are playable, turn over the top card of the stock. If this, too, is not playable, place it face-up to form the base of a waste pile. The top card of the waste pile is also available for play. You may play the Jacks from the end of the spiral as they are needed. As reserve cards are used up, replace them with a card either from the stock or the waste pile. The waste pile can be turned over to provide a new stock pile, but this can only be done once.

Reserve

Stock

Waste pile

Demon

This popular form of Patience Is called Canfield in the US, after the American in whose Saratoga gambling saloon it was invented.

Aim: *To complete four complete sequences in suit and numerical order, from base cards all of the same rank.*

Odds: *Against*

Procedure: Use a single 52-card pack. Deal 13 cards face-down in one pile, turn the pile face-up and place it at your left to form the stock. Deal the fourteenth card face-up and place it above and to the right of the stock pile. This is the first foundation card.

Deal four more cards face-up in a row below and to the right of the stock, with the first card directly under the first foundation card. These cards form the layout.

Play: The other three foundation cards are those cards which have the same pip-value as the first foundation card. Place them next to the first, face-up, as they are turned up.

The 34 cards remaining after the stock, first foundation card, and layout cards have been dealt are placed face-down, below the layout. These form the hand. Its top three cards are turned over together and laid alongside the hand, to form the waste pile. Only the top card of these three is available. If playable, it can be played on to a foundation pile or on to the layout, and the card beneath then becomes available. If not playable, it forms the first card of the waste pile. Exposed cards in the layout are also playable. Once all possible cards have been played, three more cards from the hand are turned over together and placed on top of the waste pile.

When the hand is exhausted, the waste pile is turned over, without being shuffled, and becomes the new hand, with cards taken from it in sets of three as before. This can be repeated indefinitely (sometimes it is restricted to three times only).

Foundation piles are built up in suit sequence from the foundation card (e.g. 9, 10, J, Q, K, A, 2, 3, 4, 5, 6, 7, 8).

Overlapping layout piles are built up in the sequence of next-lowest rank and opposite colour (e.g. black Seven on top of red Eight). A layout sequence can only be moved as a unit, on to a card of the next highest rank and the opposite colour to the bottom card of the unit.

Spaces occurring in the layout must be filled from the top card of the stock, or from the top of the waste pile if the stock is exhausted.

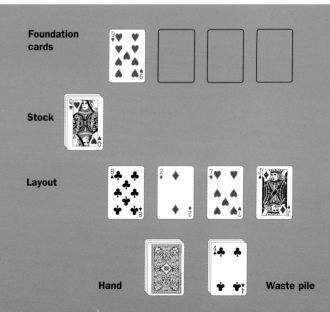

Flower Garden

This Patience has an attractive layout.

Aim: *To build up each suit in ascending sequence starting from its Ace (low Ace).*

Odds: *Even*

Procedure: Use a single 52-card pack and deal 36 cards, face-up, in six columns of six, overlapping. These are your Garden. The bottom card of each column is available for play.

Deal the remaining 16 cards in a face-up row. This is your Bouquet, and all cards in it are available at any time.

Play: As Aces become available, place them in a row above the Garden, face-up, and build up on them from Two to King in each suit. You can also add cards to the exposed cards of the Garden, in descending sequence of alternating colour (e.g. black Seven on red Eight). Empty spaces in the Garden can be filled with any exposed card or sequential set from the Garden, or any card from the Bouquet.

Note 1: The game comes out more often if you make the descending sequence in numerical order regardless of colour.

1. As dealt

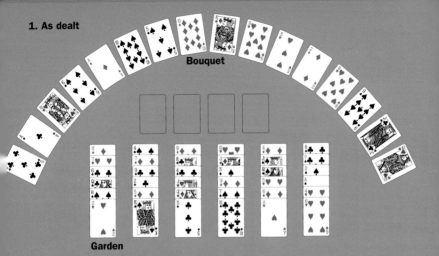

Bouquet

Garden

2. Into the game

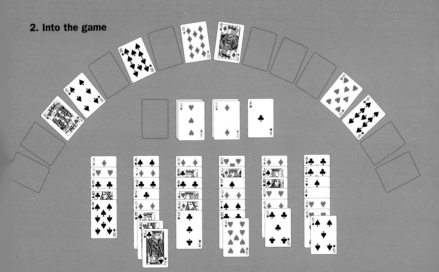

Castles in Spain

Aim: *To build up four suits, in sequence, from Aces as foundation cards, to Kings.*

Odds: *Favourable*

Procedure: Use a single 52-card pack. Deal a row of five cards, laying them face-down from left to right. Above this row lay a row of four cards, then a row of three above that. Finally place one card above the centre card of the row of three. Then deal two further cards, also face-down, on top of each of the first 13 cards. You have 13 cards left. Lay them face-up, one by one, on top of the existing piles to form the layout.

Play: All 13 upcards are available. Any Aces are taken out and set out in a foundation

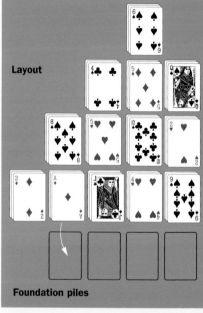

Layout

Foundation piles

row, face-up. The card beneath is turned up and becomes available for play. Available cards may be played either on to their foundation pile, or in descending sequence of alternate colour on another depot pile. Sequences or part sequences may be moved from one depot pile to another or to fill any spaces created. A vacancy made by clearing a pile may be filled with any available card. The cards may not be redealt.

Canfield

A well-known and widely played Patience game.

Aim: *To build up on each foundation card in suit and sequence, Ace (low) to King.*

Odds: *Against*

Procedure: Use a single 52-card pack. Deal one card face-up and six others face-down in a single row, left to right. Deal a card face-up on top of the second card, then five face-down on top of the others. Deal a card face-up on the third pile, and another four face-down, and continue in this way until you have seven piles. Remaining cards are placed in a packet, face-down, to form the stock.

Play: Aces are placed in a row as the foundation cards, separate from the seven piles, as they appear. Cards transferred to their foundation piles may not be moved again. Within the layout, build descending sequences of alternate colour (e.g. red Ten on black Jack). These may be moved as a unit. Spaces in the layout may be filled only with a King. If no more cards can be moved, turn over the top card of the stock. If it is not usable, put it face up on the waste pile. When the stock is used up, turn the waste pile over to form the stock, but only once.

Foundation piles

Stock   **Waste pile**

Shamrocks

Aim: *To build four complete suit sequences from Ace to King, on the foundation piles.*

Odds: *Against*

Procedure: Use a single 52-card pack. Deal all the cards into 17 sets of three and spread them out in fan-shapes so that suit and pip-value are clearly visible. Arrange your fans in three slightly curved rows of seven, six and four respectively, to make the whole layout into a fan shape. There will be one single card left. This too goes face-up on the layout, below the fans. If you have a King and another card of the same suit in any of your fans, put the King below the other. Uncovered cards are available for play.

Play: No fan is allowed to hold more than three cards, so the first move must be to add a card to the single card. Within the layout, a card can only be added to a fan if it is in the same suit, and the next down in rank, from the top card. Aces, as they become available, should be moved to form the bases of the four foundation piles on to which you build up a sequence from Ace to King in each suit. When you have moved all the cards out of a fan, the space remains empty. Cards cannot be moved from foundation piles back into the layout.

Variant: A simpler form is Lovely Lucy, where the odds are rather more in favour of a successful outcome. Procedure is as for Shamrocks, but Kings are left where they are. If you have no cards that can be moved, you are allowed to gather up all remaining cards in the layout, shuffle them, and re-deal. Two re-deals are permitted. If, after two re-deals, you still come to a block, you may as a grace take any one card from anywhere in the layout and move it either to a foundation pile or to elsewhere in the layout.

Foundation piles

Maria

This is a very tough game to resolve.

Aim: *To release the eight Aces and build sequences in suit on them, up to Kings.*

Odds: *Against*

Procedure: Use two packs of 52 cards. Deal out 36 cards face-up in four columns of nine overlapping cards each. This forms the layout.

Play: The rest of the combined pack forms the stock, which should be placed face-down. If any of the exposed cards in the layout are Aces, move them to the foundation row. If any exposed cards can be built on the foundation cards, move them accordingly. Start with Twos and remember to follow suit. Turn the top card of the stock over. If it is an Ace, put it on the foundation row. If it can be built on to the foundation piles in suit and sequence, do so. If it can be placed on an exposed card in the layout, to begin a sequence in descending order and alternating colour (e.g. red Nine on top of black Ten, then black Eight), do so. Otherwise start a waste pile, face-up, of which the top card is always available for play. Only one card can be moved at a time; sequences cannot be moved. When a column becomes empty, any available card may be used to fill the space. Once the combined pack is used up, there is no re-deal.

Variant: There is also a version of this game known as Midshipman. In this, the first 18 cards of the layout are dealt face-down. You can then turn over the downcards as they become exposed. Maria is more interesting. In Patience, the more cards you can see, the more you have to use your judgement.

Foundation row

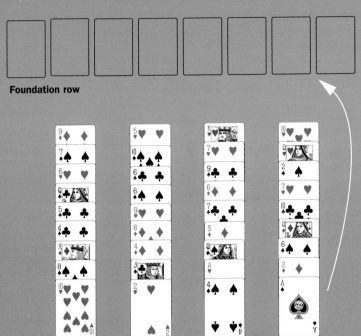

Layout

Stock   **Waste pile**

Alternate

This is one of a range of games said by some authorities to stem from the original form of Patience.

Aim: *To build suits in numerical sequence but alternating colour up from the two red Aces to the Kings, and down from the two black Kings to the Aces.*

Odds: *Even*

Procedure: Use a single pack of 52 cards. Extract the two red Aces and the two black Kings, and set them down, face-up, as foundation cards. There is no deal as such. The rest of the pack is placed face-down to form your stock.

Play: Turn over the top card of the stock. If it can be played to one of the foundation piles, do so (e.g. if it is a Two of Clubs, you could place it on the Ace of Hearts or of Diamonds, face-up; if it is a Queen of Hearts, place it on the King of Spades or of Clubs). If the top card cannot be played to a foundation pile, use it to start the first of four waste piles, face-up. The top cards of the waste piles are also available to play. Continue turning over the stock, building sequences or playing to the waste piles, until you have completed all the foundation piles, or you are blocked.

If you use up all the stock, you can gather up the four waste piles and turn them over in a single face-down pile as the new stock. This can only be done once.

Top cards may not be transferred between the waste piles.

1. Early in the game

Foundation row

Stock

Waste piles

2. As the game progresses

Foundation row

Stock

Waste piles

Terrace

Unlike other forms of Patience, this builds on the foundation cards in alternating colours, not suit.

Aim: *To build up eight sequences, from selected base cards, in alternating colours.*

Odds: *Favourable*

Procedure: Use two packs of 52 cards. Deal 11 cards face-up in an overlapping row. This is the 'terrace' and forms a reserve. Deal four cards, face-up, side by side in a row below the terrace. Select one of these as your foundation card number – e.g. Four – and place it to start a separate foundation card row. Deal further cards to bring the second row up to nine cards. This forms your layout.

Play: Turn the rest of the combined pack face-down to form the stock. The available cards are the exposed card at the right-hand end of the terrace, and the cards in the layout. Look at the layout and move any available cards to the foundation row. Fill resulting gaps in the layout from the stock. If the next card is a foundation card, move it straight to the foundation row and deal another to the layout. If the exposed card in the terrace is a foundation card, move it to the foundation row, but do not replace it with another card. Cards from the terrace can only be moved into the foundation piles, not into the layout.

Sequences may be assembled on the cards in the layout, in descending numerical order and alternating colours only (e.g. black Seven on red Eight, followed by red Six). Gaps in the layout can be filled only by the top card of the stock or the waste pile.

When you have made all possible moves, continue play by turning over cards from the stock, one by one. These can be played either to

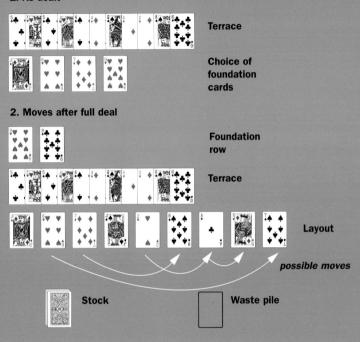

1. As dealt

Terrace

Choice of
foundation
cards

2. Moves after full deal

Foundation
row

Terrace

Layout

possible moves

Stock

Waste pile

the foundation piles, or the layout, if they fit the required sequence.
Otherwise they should be played to a waste pile, of which the top card
will always be available for play. No re-deal is allowed in this game.
Note 1: If you deal two or more cards of the same rank among the
four from which you choose the foundation cards, you may select
these and simply deal extra cards to make the layout up to nine.
Note 2: The choice of foundation card can affect the outcome: look
closely at the four possible cards and the terrace before choosing,
and pick the base card on which you can build most easily.

Colonel

This game is also known as Uncle Walter's. One card games expert describes it as 'horrible', and it's certainly challenging.

Aim: *To release the Aces and build up on them in suit and sequence to the Kings.*

Odds: *Against*

Procedure: Use two 52-card packs. Deal three rows of 12 cards, making 12 columns of three cards, not overlapping.

Play: The rest of the combined packs forms the stock. Turn this face-down, and turn over the top card. If it is an Ace, place it to start a row of foundation cards. Only the bottom row of cards in the layout is available to play at first. As cards are turned over from the stock, they can be added to the layout if they fit, in descending order of the same suit, on an available card. Unplayable cards should be discarded to form a waste pile, whose top card is also available for play.

Other cards become available when there is a gap in the row below them. If any Aces in the layout are exposed, move them out to the row of foundation cards. Move other exposed cards in order to build on the Aces (starting with a Two of the same suit), or to make sequences on available cards in the layout in descending numerical order of the same suit. If a column is emptied, a card from the stock should be dealt to the space. Only one card at a time may be moved. Sequences cannot be moved. No re-deal is allowed.

Note: Sequences in the layout should be laid out in piles rather than in overlapping columns. You are allowed to look through the cards in any such pile to remind yourself of its contents.

Foundation row

Layout

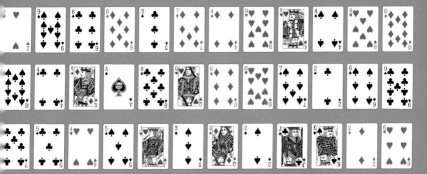

Stock

Waste pile

2D and 3D can be moved to their foundation pile
Move 5S on to 6S to release AS to foundation row
2S and 3S can be played to foundation row
JH can be played to QH
10H can be played to JH
9H can be played to 10H
New card to column 8, and on you go . . .

Hemispheres

This is a nineteenth-century game, typical of the period in its complexity.

Aim: *To form four Ace–King and four King–Ace sequences, in suit.*
Odds: *Favourable*

Procedure: Use two packs of 52 cards. Extract the four black Kings and place them in a North–South, West–East formation, one suit N–S, the other W–E. Also extract the four red Aces, and place them to extend the cross pattern, in the same opposing positions. At the North end of the cross, place an Ace of Spades, at the West, a King of Hearts, at the South an Ace of Clubs, and at the East a King of Diamonds. These are the barrier cards. Deal 12 cards to complete a circle round the cross pattern, three in each quadrant between the red Kings and black Aces, starting with the West to North quadrant. The remaining cards form the stock.
Play: The eight cards forming the cross pattern are foundation cards. Following suit and sequence, you build down from Kings to Aces, and up from Aces to Kings. The barrier cards complete the sequences, and are not touched in the game. The 12 cards in the quadrants form the layout, and all are available. But before they can be used for building, they must be in their correct hemisphere – red cards in the northern hemisphere and black cards in the southern hemisphere. Cards can be exchanged on a one-for-one basis between the two hemispheres.

On the layout, cards can be moved on to others as follows: black cards in suit and ascending sequence; red cards in suit and descending sequence. Cards may also be moved on to the foundation piles, in sequence. When all possible moves have been completed, take further cards from the stock to fill vacant spaces in the quadrants.

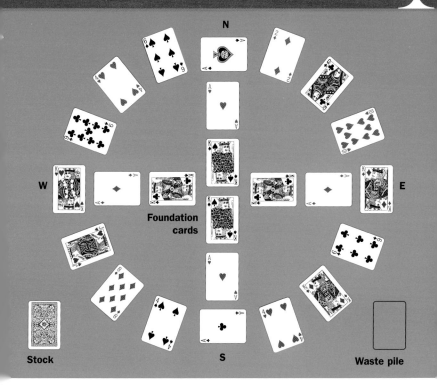

When you have no more playable cards in the full layout, turn over the top card of the stock. Play the card on to the layout or foundation piles, if possible. Otherwise discard it as the start of a waste pile, and turn over another card from the stock. The top card of the waste pile is always available. If you reach a point where there are no cards left either in the stock or the waste pile, and there is a card trapped in the wrong hemisphere, it is permissible to transfer it to a vacant place in the right hemisphere, without an exchange. The waste pile can be turned over once and used as a stock pile, when the stock pile is used up.

Four Winds

Aim: *To build up four suits in sequence from Aces to Kings, and four down from Kings to Aces.*

Odds: *Against*

Procedure: Use two packs of 52 cards, shuffled thoroughly into a single pack. Set out a layout as follows: lay down the first card, face up, tilted on its long side, and make a column of four separated face-up cards, normally placed, below it. At the foot of a column place another card face-up, tilting upwards on its long side. Leaving a space of about 16 inches, set out another column as a mirror-image of the first. Now you have two columns of four cards, plus four corner cards. If any of these first 12 cards is a King or Ace, move them into the central space as foundation cards. Replace them in the layout with other cards from the stock.

In the central area, the piles are laid out in four rows of four; Kings in the upper two rows, Aces in the lower two.

Play: You now want to build your piles in each suit – upwards from the Aces in numerical sequence (next card required is a Two), downwards from the Kings (next card required is a Queen). Any corner cards which can be transferred to foundation piles may be moved immediately. Cards from the layout columns can only be moved to the foundation piles if they are on the same row as the foundation pile.

Replace any gaps using cards from the stock. Repeat the procedure as before, and continue until you have used up all the stock. If you are blocked at this point, reshuffle and start over again.

Once you have no more stock cards, you can move cards freely within the layout and foundation piles. Cards may be moved from any point in the layout on to any appropriate foundation pile. You can also build ascending or descending sequences on layout and corner cards, for transference to foundation piles.

If you are blocked at this stage, you may take up the corner and layout cards, in the order in which you laid them down, and re-deal them without shuffling. This will reverse their order, turning any sequences round the other way. You may do this re-deal twice in the course of any one game.

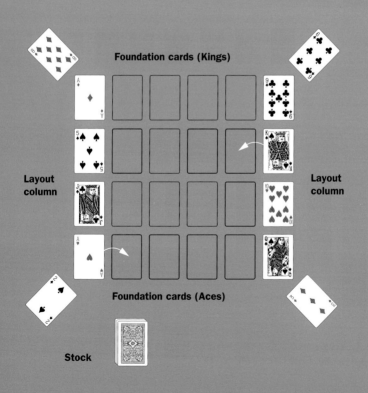

Backbone

Aim: *To use the Aces as foundation cards and build up a sequence, in suit, to Kings.*

Odds: *Against*

Procedure: Use two packs of 52 cards. Deal 11 pairs of cards face-up in a double column making a succession of V-shapes. Each side should not touch the other, but the cards within each side may overlap each other. Lay the twelfth card on its long side, face up, at the bottom of the double column. If it turns out to be a King, replace it somewhere in the pack and deal another card. This represents the backbone. Now place the ribs – four cards on each side, laid on their long sides. The rib cards are the layout, and the backbone cards are the reserve.

Play: Start by moving any available Aces to the foundation row, and replace them from the stock. Available cards can then be built on the Aces in the correct sequence, following suit. Cards can be built in suits in descending sequence on the rib cards. The single card at the base of the backbone is the only one of the reserve available to start with; once it has been played, the two bottom cards of the V arrangement are available, and so on up. Cards from the reserve are used to replace gaps in the layout.

Once the reserve is used up, or no further moves are possible, turn cards over from stock, placing them face-up in a waste pile if they cannot be used. The top card of the waste pile is available. The waste pile can be turned over once and used as a stock pile, when the stock pile is used up.

As Aces emerge from the stock, they are placed immediately in the foundation row.

Reserve (backbone cards)

**Layout
(rib cards)**

**Layout
(rib cards)**

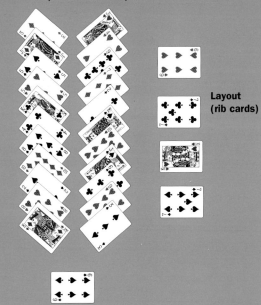

Foundation row

Stock **Waste pile**

Ladder

Aim: *To make eight foundation piles using the Aces and Kings, building from Aces up to Kings, in suit; and from Kings down to Aces, in suit.*

Odds: *Even*

Procedure: Use two packs of 52 cards. Deal four cards, face-up and without overlapping, in a column on the left side of your table, and then four on the right. Between the two columns is the space in which you will place the Ace and King foundation cards. They are set horizontally to represent the 'rungs' of the ladder. Below this upper part of the layout, deal 24 cards in six sets of four, arranged so that one card is exposed but the values of all can be seen.

Play: Any playable Aces and Kings may be transferred to start off the foundation piles. Cards can be taken from the 'sides' of the ladder or from the available cards of the six spreads. Spaces made do not have to be filled immediately, unless you have removed all four cards from one side of the ladder, in which case you must replace them with available cards from the spreads. If there is a single vacancy in one of the ladder sides, you can fill it from any of the two top cards in any of the spreads. If there are two vacancies, each can be filled from any one of the top three cards of any spread. Doing this at the right moment can free up cards for playing to the foundation piles.

The sets of four cards are not replaced as they are used up, but when all playable cards have been moved, deal a further six sets of four cards, and play on. Repeat until you have used all the cards of the combined pack. You may now gather up the remaining spreads, in the order in which you dealt them, and reform them into a new pack. This re-deal can only be done once.

Stock

Virginia Reel

Aim: *To set out 24 foundation cards and build up from them in suit and specific numerical sequences as follows: 2, 5, 8, J; 3, 6, 9, Q; 4, 7, 10, K.*

Odds: *Against*

Procedure: Use two 52-card packs. Extract any Two, any Three and any Four from the pack, and lay them in a column, face-up, not overlapping. These are your first foundation cards. The 21 other Twos, Threes and Fours are the other foundation cards. Deal seven cards, face-up, in a row to the right of each first foundation card.

Play: Your aim is to get all the Twos, Threes and Fours into their respective foundation rows: top row for Twos, middle for Threes and lowest for Fours. Then you build up from them in the sequences described under 'Aim', above.

First examine the cards to see if any building can be done. Cards may only be built into a foundation pile when they are in the appropriate row (i.e. horizontal line) for that pile, and of course they must be of the same suit, and three ranks above, the cards on which they are placed. Any Aces dealt into the layout can be taken out and set aside. The resulting gap can be filled by moving a foundation card which is in an inappropriate row. Foundation cards can also be moved into gaps caused by building. If you have two rows each containing foundation cards belonging to the other, you may exchange them, or do a triple exchange involving a Two, Three and Four.

When no more moves are possible, deal a further row of eight cards, face-up, as a reserve. Lay aside any Aces, as before, and replace them with usable cards. Any foundation cards in the reserve may be moved into their appropriate rows. Cards may be built from the reserve into foundation piles only if they are in the correct row. When no further moves are possible, deal a further eight cards to the reserve, either filling gaps or overlapping on the lower card, so that the reserve begins to form columns stretching towards you. Only exposed cards may be played, on the same basis as before. Once the two packs are used up, there is no re-deal. To help out, there is one grace. You may take one card from anywhere in the reserve, and add it to a foundation row.

Note: In some forms of the game, Aces can only be moved out when there is a correct foundation card to replace them with, either from the reserve or from another row. If from another row, the resulting gap must also be filled by a correct foundation card.

Further foundation cards

First foundation cards

Remove AS. Move 4S to bottom row. Move 3H to middle row. Exchange 4H in top row and 2D in bottom row.

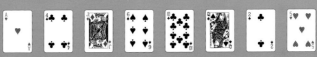

First row of reserve

Remove AH. Move 4C to bottom row.

Blind Patience

The unusual feature of this tricky game is that the layout cards are dealt face-down. Careful judgement is required when moving cards.

Aim: *To release all eight Aces and build up from them in suit and sequence to the Kings.*

Odds: *Against*

Procedure: Use two 52-card packs. Deal four rows of ten cards each, face-down. Let the cards in each column overlap, with the last cards exposed (though face-down).

Play: The rest of the combined pack forms the stock. Turn cards from the stock over, one by one, and decide what to do with each. Aces should be laid face-up in a row as foundation cards. Any cards which can be built directly on to the Aces, beginning with Twos (in the appropriate suit), should be moved to the appropriate foundation pile.

Other cards may either be moved into a single waste pile, face-up, of which the top card is always available for play; or may be added, face-up, at the end of any column of face-down cards in the layout. You can then use these cards to make sequences in descending order and alternating suits (e.g. starting with a red Jack, you could add a black Ten, then a red Nine, and so on).

You may turn over the exposed face-down card in any column and build with it, or assemble a sequence on it. Sequences may not be transferred as one, but the exposed card at the end of a sequence may be moved to any other column as the top (i.e. exposed) card.

When a column has been completely emptied, the space can be filled by any available card.

There is no re-deal. Once you have dealt out all the cards, and can find no more possible moves, you may turn over the end cards of any column which are still face-down, and use them if they are playable. Otherwise, they stay in position.

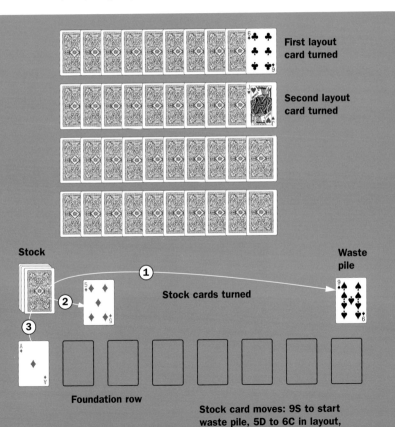

First layout card turned

Second layout card turned

Stock

Waste pile

(1)

Stock cards turned

(2)

(3)

Foundation row

Stock card moves: 9S to start waste pile, 5D to 6C in layout, AD to foundation row

Miss Milligan

This popular Patience is often tricky to resolve.

Aim: *To build eight sequences in suit from Ace up to King.*
Odds: *Against*

Procedure: Use two packs of 52 cards. Deal eight cards from the pack in a row from left to right, face-down. Deal a second row of eight cards, face-down, overlapping the first row, and a third row face-up.
Play: If you have dealt any Aces, take them from the layout and place them above the layout row as foundation cards. Move cards in the layout either to the foundation piles, if they fit, or within the layout by starting sequences in descending numerical order and alternating colour. When you have no more cards to move, deal a further eight, overlapping any columns that have been formed. Again, move cards as their suit and value allow, into the foundation piles or layout columns. Cards may be moved singly or as sequences. If a space is created by the transfer of a whole column, the space can be filled only by a King, or a sequence that includes a King; if none is available, it will be filled by a card from the next deal. Continue to deal and move until all the cards have been dealt. Then complete all possible moves.

If you have not resolved the game, a grace is allowed at this point. Any exposed card can be taken out and held in reserve, enabling you to play the card that was beneath it, and to continue with any possible further moves after that. This move is known as 'waiving' or 'weaving'. The reserve card must be returned to the layout by being placed on an exposed card of the opposite colour and of the next rank upwards (e.g. a red Eight on a black Nine). If you cannot do this, the game is lost. If you can do this, you are allowed to waive again,

First deal

Moves

Second deal

Moves

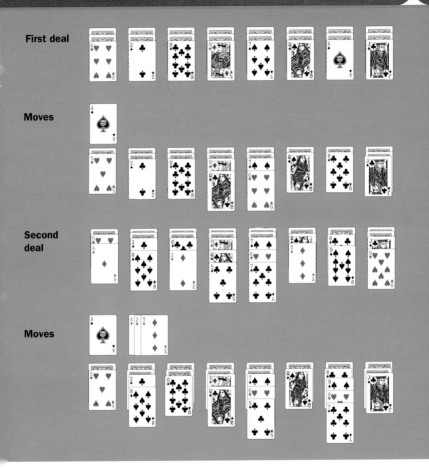

and repeat the same procedure as often as necessary to resolve the game.

Variation: Another form omits the two face-down rows of eight cards from the layout, starting with just one row of eight face-up cards.

King Albert

**Named after the popular and sporty
king of the Belgians, who was killed in
a climbing accident in 1934.**

Aim: *To build up each suit in ascending sequence from its Ace
(Aces are low).*
Odds: *Even*

Procedure: Use one pack of 52 cards. Deal a row of nine cards, face-
up, then a row of eight (which starts on the second card of the first
row and overlaps with it), then a row of seven (which starts on the
second card of the second row and overlaps with it). Continue in
diminishing rows, always starting one card to the right, until you end
with a ninth row of just one card.

The seven remaining cards should be laid out, face-up, in a row
below the layout. These form your reserve.
Play: All the exposed cards, and the reserve cards, are available for
play. Remove any exposed Aces and set them out in a row as
foundation cards. Build any appropriate exposed cards on to the
Aces, starting with Twos.

Cards in the layout can be moved from column to column (if
exposed), to form downward sequences of alternating colour (e.g.
black Seven on red Eight, followed by red Six). When a column is
completely emptied, the space may be filled by any available card.
Cards that have been played to the foundation piles can be
temporarily transferred back, from the top of a pile only, into the
layout, either to add to a column or to fill a gap.
Variant: Only one card may be moved at a time.

Layout as dealt:

Layout

Reserve

After a few moves:

Now transfer KD to col 1,
AH to foundation pile, QC
to KD, JH to QC. 6D to
7S, and on you go . . .

Spider

A problematic one to work out, and with many possible variants, this game has associations with President Franklin D. Roosevelt, who was a keen Patience player.

Aim: *To build eight sequences downwards in suit from King to Ace.*
Odds: *Against*

Procedure: Use two packs of 52 cards. Deal ten cards face-down in a row. Now deal three more cards on each of the original ten cards, dealing each row at a time. This makes ten piles of four. Now deal ten further cards on top of the piles, face-up. This forms your layout.
Play: Look at the face-up cards, and move them from one column to another to create descending numerical sequences. You can only move a sequence from one column to another if all the cards in it are of the same suit. But it may be placed on a card of a different suit, so long as the numerical order is maintained. As face-down cards become exposed, you can turn them over and play them. If there is nowhere to move them, they block the rest of the pile.

A column that is completely emptied may be filled with any available card or single-suit sequence. Kings may not be moved, except into empty column spaces. Once you have made a complete suit sequence, from King to Ace, in the layout, you can remove it, and place it in a pile to one side. You don't have do this as soon as the sequence is completed.

When you have made all possible moves, deal another ten cards, face-up, one on each column, and repeat the play as before. Continue until all the cards have been dealt, and no more moves can be made, either because you have completed the game or have become blocked.

Layout as dealt:

After moves:

Second deal:

After moves:

Index of Games